A·GUIDE
to YOUR OWN
MiNi COO-RIER

Written by
Sarah Royal

T0364023

RP Minis®
Hachette Book Group
1290 Avenue of the Americas, New York, NY 10104
www.runningpress.com
@Running_Press

First Edition: April 2023

Published by RP Minis, an imprint of Perseus Books, LLC, a
subsidiary of Hachette Book Group, Inc. The RP Minis name
and logo is a registered trademark of the Hachette Book Group.

The publisher is not responsible for websites (or their content)
that are not owned by the publisher.

ISBN: 978-0-7624-8230-6

CONTENTS

INTRODUCTION

Imagine yourself in an office.

Perhaps it's in a labyrinthine, multistory commercial building with felt cubicle walls or a start-up-style space with copious amounts of white boards and free granola bars. Maybe it's a classroom full of piles of books or a nurses' station at the hospital. It could even be your home office, adjacent to both your roommate's home office desk and the dresser where you keep your hard pants that you no longer wear.

Wherever your office location, you'd be hard-pressed to survive the stress of work without communicating with, venting to, or just plain gossiping with a fellow workmate. And to get a chat brewing, you'll want to send that person a little message.

It may surprise you that the best way to do that isn't by phone, or email, or even fax. **It's by messenger pigeon.**

All About the Noble—
and Oft Maligned—Pigeon

In many cities across the globe, pigeons are not-so-affectionately referred to as "rats with wings." But most people would be surprised to learn that a pigeon is, essentially, a dove. Yes, that white, heavenly, pure bird present at many a wedding as a symbol of peace and love is essentially the same bird we're used to seeing peck at dropped food and defecating on car windshields.

Around 5,000 years ago, Mesopotamians started housing and taming the rock dove (*Columba livia*), breeding them for food where other animals had become scarce. Many years later, Europeans brought pigeons along with them on their travels, and the birds escaped. And then they *thrived*.

Today, cities around the globe are bursting at the seams with pigeons. Pigeons can eat human food—basically *any* food—unlike other birds. They evolved from nesting on rocky seaside cliffs to nesting atop air-conditioner units, fire escapes,

awnings, and other city-centric landscapes that mimic those cliffs. They're also not particularly concerned about moving quickly to get away from a moving car or from underfoot.

Perhaps most importantly, though, is that they can easily navigate through a complex cityscape. That's where the "messenger" part of the Messenger Pigeon comes in.

After hanging out with (and chowing down on) pigeons for a while, people realized they were actually quite good at homing. Soon, they began sending messages tucked away into tubes secured to the pigeon's legs or neck—a safe, timely, and largely undetected manner of exchanging information. Ancient Greeks, Genghis Khan, and Mediterranean sailors all used pigeons in this way. Even Noah in the Bible sends a pigeon out from the ark to seek dry land.

Scientists today theorize that pigeons use all sorts of methods of navigation, including their sense of smell, following man-made roads, or even sensing the earth's magnetic field. Whatever the method, pigeons have proven that they're one of the most docile, easily trained avian aviators out there.

Today, pigeons are one of the few breeds

of wildlife, alongside squirrels and seagulls, that people can still regularly interact with in most urban environments. Thanks to your Mini Office Messenger Pigeon, that now includes the office.

A Pithy Pigeon Profile

- Grows typically up to 14 inches
- Wingspan typically reaches up to 26 inches
- Weight typically reaches up to 13 ounces
- Color is variable
- White rump
- Rounded tail
- Bobs head
- Can sleep with one eye open
- Typically mate for life
- Can cover round-trip flights of up to 100 miles
- One of the most intelligent birds on the planet

Famous Pigeons in History

There have been many famous fans of pigeons throughout history, such as Pablo Picasso, Nikola Tesla, and Elvis Presley. But there also have been famous *pigeons* throughout history, too, celebrated for their speed, station, and service:

CHER AMI

During World War I, a military pigeon named Cher Ami was the last chance the French commander of the 77th Infantry Division had to tell headquarters that they were surrounded by German troops. Cher

Ami was shot in both the chest and the leg but delivered the message successfully, saving the lives of the soldiers.

THE "PIGEON POST" STAFF

During the Franco-Prussian War, Prussians had full control of all telegraph and postal services in Paris, France. Parisians set up a "pigeon post" to carry both official and private communication all over France, with an estimated 1 million messages sent over just four months.

WINKIE

A British bomber was shot down during World War II and stranded its crew in a dinghy in the North Sea. They tied a message with their approximate coordinates around the leg of a pigeon named Winkie, who flew 129 miles to the Scottish coast. A rescue boat soon arrived and the whole crew survived.

BOLT

The world's fastest racing pigeon, appropriately named Bolt, was sold by a Belgian breeder to a Chinese businessman for nearly half a million dollars in 2013. Bolt was famous for flying in long-distance pigeon races, reaching speeds of up to 100 miles per hour.

How to Use Your Mini Office Messenger Pigeon

The next time you want to gab with your coworker, consider your Mini Office Messenger Pigeon. Sure, in this modern world, we have email, text message, phone calls, instant messaging, and interoffice memorandums—but your messenger pigeon is far superior to any of these options.

No one can overhear your pigeon message by accident. You can't accidentally send the message to the wrong person—so long as you know what desk to place it on—and you can't accidentally leave a memo on the copy machine.

Choose one of the included common office messages here, or tear out a blank sheet and write your own. Then tuck it under the professional and primed plumage of your Mini Office Messenger Pigeon inside its messenger bag, stroll over to your intended recipient, and simply place the pigeon at a place of your choosing. Then walk away swiftly yet casually, pretending your true engagement was with the half a doughnut left in the breakroom. You and your messaging compatriot will enjoy endless hours of exchanging clever communiqués.

Enjoy this wonderful way to pass the time as you glide through the minutiae of office life, before the clock strikes five and you fly the coop.

Let's do happy hour tonight

I'm ready for lunch. You?

Meet in breakroom in 5

Coffee time!

We need to debrief

Let's take this offline

Is it Friday yet?

**Come to my
desk ASAP**

Just saying hi!

Cookies in the breakroom

Check your inbox!

Did you hear the news?

Nice pitch today!

Let's plan our escape?

Need to share
cute pics of
my dog

Seriously,
who put them
in charge?